For my parents
with love

First published in Great Britain 1995
by Methuen Children's Books
an imprint of Reed Consumer Books Ltd
Michelin House, 81 Fulham Road, London SW3 6RB
and Auckland, Melbourne, Singapore and Toronto

Illustrations © Belinda Downes 1995
Arrangements © Reed International Books Ltd 1995

A CIP catalogue record for this title
is available from the British Library

ISBN 0 416 19100 2

Produced by Mandarin Offset
Printed and bound in Singapore

silent night

with
embroideries by
Belinda Downes

Methuen

Silent Night

Si — lent Night! Ho — ly Night!
All is calm, all is bright. 'Round yon
vir — gin mo — ther and child! Ho — ly In — fant, so
ten — der and mild, Sleep in hea — ven — ly pea —
— ce, Sle — ep in hea — ve — nly peace.

Silent Night! Holy Night!
Shepherds quake at the sight!
Glories stream from heaven afar,
Heav'nly hosts sing, "Alleluia!"
Christ, the Saviour, is born!
Christ, the Saviour, is born!

Silent Night! Holy Night!
Son of God, love's pure light!
Radiant beams from Thy holy face,
With the dawn of redeeming grace,
Jesus, Lord at Thy birth,
Jesus, Lord at Thy birth.

O Christmas Tree

And, oh, the Christmas tree can be
A source of simple pleasure:
To every girl and every boy
It speaks of holidays and joy:
Ah, yes, the Christmas tree can be
A source of simple pleasure.

Hark! The Herald Angels Sing

Christ, by highest heav'n adored,
Christ, the everlasting Lord;
Late in time behold Him come,
Offspring of the favoured one.
Veiled in flesh, the Godhead see!
Hail, th'incarnate Deity!
Pleased as man with man to dwell,
Jesus, our Emmanuel.
Hark! the herald angels sing,
"Glory to the newborn King."

Hail the heaven-born Prince of peace!
Hail the Sun of Righteousness!
Light and life to all He brings,
Risen with healing in His wings;
Mild He lays His glory by,
Born that man no more may die,
Born to raise the sons of earth,
Born to give them second birth.
Hark! the herald angels sing,
"Glory to the newborn King."

Ding Dong! Merrily On High

E'en so here below, below,
Let steeple bells be swungen,
And i-o, i-o, i-o,
By priest and people sungen:
Gloria, Hosanna in excelsis!

Pray you dutifully prime
Your matin chime, ye ringers;
May you beautifully rime
Your eve-time song ye singers:
Gloria, Hosanna in excelsis!

Away In A Manger

The cattle are lowing, the baby awakes,
But little Lord Jesus, no crying He makes.
I love Thee, Lord Jesus, look down from the sky,
And stay by my cradle, till morning is nigh.

Be near me, Lord Jesus; I ask Thee to stay
Close by me forever, and love me, I pray.
Bless all the dear children in Thy tender care,
And fit us for heaven, to live with Thee there.

O Come, All Ye Faithful

Adeste, Fideles,
Laeti triumphantes,
Venite, venite in Bethlehem;
Natum videte,
Regem angelorum:
Venite adoremus,
Venite adoremus,
Venite adoremus,
Dominum.

Sing choirs of Angels,
Sing in exultation,
Sing all ye citizens of heav'n above:
Glory to God in the highest:
O come, let us adore Him,
O come, let us adore Him,
O come, let us adore Him,
Christ, the Lord.

Angels We Have Heard On High

An–gels we have heard on high, Sweet–ly sing–ing o'er the plains;

And the moun–tains in re–ply E – cho–ing their joy – ous strains.

Glor — ia

in ex – cel – sis De — o. Glor —

— ia in ex – cel – sis De — o.

Shepherds, why this jubilee?
Why your joyous songs prolong?
What the gladsome tidings be
Which inspire your heavenly song?
Gloria in excelsis Deo.
Gloria in excelsis Deo.

Come to Bethlehem, and see
Him whose birth the angels sing;
Come adore on bended knee,
Christ, the Lord, our newborn King.
Gloria in excelsis Deo.
Gloria in excelsis Deo.

O Little Town Of Bethlehem

How silently, how silently,
The wondrous gift is given!
So God imparts to human hearts
The blessings of His heaven.
No ear may hear His coming;
But in this world of sin,
Where meek souls will receive Him, still
The dear Christ enters in.

O holy Child of Bethlehem,
Descend to us, we pray;
Cast out our sin, and enter in:
Be born in us today.
We hear the Christmas angels
The great glad tidings tell:
O come to us, abide with us,
Our Lord Emmanuel.

Joy To The World!

Joy to the world! The Saviour reigns;
Let men their songs employ;
While fields and floods, rocks, hills and
  plains,
Repeat the sounding joy,
Repeat the sounding joy,
Repeat, repeat the sounding joy.

He rules the world with truth and grace,
And makes the nations prove
The glories of His righteousness,
And wonders of His love,
And wonders of His love,
And wonders, and wonders of His love.

Once In Royal David's City

He came down to earth from heaven,
Who is God and Lord of all,
And His shelter was a stable,
And His cradle was a stall;
With the poor, and mean, and lowly,
Lived on earth our Saviour holy.

Not in that poor lowly stable,
With the oxen standing by,
We shall see Him; but in heaven,
Set at God's right hand on high;
When like stars His children crowned
All in white shall wait around.

The First Nowell

They looked up and saw a star
Shining in the east beyond them far,
And to the earth it gave great light,
And so it continued both day and night.
Nowell, Nowell, Nowell, Nowell,
Born is the King of Israel.

Then let us all with one accord
Sing praises to our heav'nly Lord,
That hath made heav'n and earth of naught,
And with His blood mankind hath bought:
Nowell, Nowell, Nowell, Nowell,
Born is the King of Israel.

I Saw Three Ships

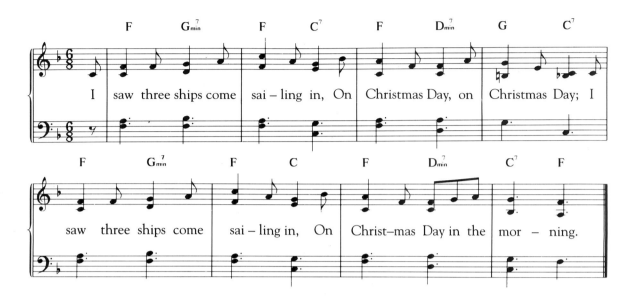

I saw three ships come sai – ling in, On Christmas Day, on Christmas Day; I
saw three ships come sai – ling in, On Christ–mas Day in the mor – ning.

And what was in those ships all three,
On Christmas Day, on Christmas Day;
And what was in those ships all three,
On Christmas Day in the morning.

The Virgin Mary and Christ were there,
On Christmas Day, on Christmas Day;
The Virgin Mary and Christ were there,
On Christmas Day in the morning.